FIRST
DIASPORIST
MANIFESTO

For Sandra, who puts me down when I complain,
replying she'd rather live in these times (as a woman
and artist) than any other

R. B. Kitaj

FIRST DIASPORIST MANIFESTO

with 60 illustrations

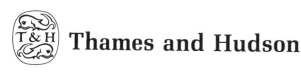 Thames and Hudson

Frontispiece *Sandra*

Illustrations courtesy Marlborough Fine Art (London) Ltd

*First published in the United States in 1989 by
Thames and Hudson Inc., 500 Fifth Avenue,
New York, New York 10110*

Library of Congress Catalog Card Number 88-51526

Printed and bound in Great Britain

CONTENTS

A modern book *On Liberty* (J. S. Mill) has maintained that from the freedom of individual men to persist in idiosyncrasies the world may be enriched. Why should we not apply this argument to the idiosyncrasy of a nation, and pause in our haste to hoot it down?

George Eliot (on the Jewish problem)

False Messiah 1985–86 (detail).
Tate Gallery Foundation, London

PROLOGUE

The poor bastard had Jew on the brain.

Philip Roth The Counterlife

Philip Roth 1985

Painting is not my life. My life is my life. Painting is a great idea I carry from place to place. It is an idea full of ideas, like a refugee's suitcase, a portable Ark of the Covenant. Before I run for my train, spilling a few of these painting ideas, I just want to stand still on the platform and announce some of my credentials (more later): I am a dislocated pretender. I play at being a refugee, at studying, at painting. All this is pretence in the sense Picasso meant when he said: 'The artist must know the manner whereby to convince others of the truthfulness of his lies.'

I offer this manifesto to Jews and non-Jews alike, in the (fairly) sure knowledge that there be a Diasporist painting – maybe in a primitive state, maybe of a different order or framework of painting thought, of painting speech. I've been studying my Jews, and so you must forgive the emphasis on them, but painting beyond Jewish concern may just prosper thereby, because, as a wise man said, you delve into your own soul and wander through all the

Self-Portrait (Cold in Paris) 1983

dimensions of the world. I believe there is a spirit or 'ego' in a people, as in a man, which compels the creativity of that people, which propels it and inspires it – openly, secretly, embarrassingly, even modestly. If my argument adopts a tribal dimension, perhaps that will be understood by the heirs of Benin, Sumer, Greece, Siena, India and the Lowlands. Even the outer spatial Frank Stella (b. 1937) speaks of his 'half-unconsciously held Mediterranean gift'.

The Jews have been called a lot of things in their four thousand off and on Diasporic years (mostly off). I keep a funny list to which I add from time to time, a list of 'traits' attributed to Jews. Aggrieved, hated and admired are on my list. I'm not saying that any painter who feels aggrieved, hated and admired can be a Diasporist, but the closer a volume of traits homes in on a painting, the more distinctive the visual effect I would guess – no? Excuse me, I may miss my manifesto-express. Quickly then – I'm glad many Jews settled in a nation-state of their own. It is a precarious, daring refuge, full of sweet and awful vision. Israel was formed by specifically Jewish structures of mind, biblical and other history, and enigma variations (such as flourishing Jew-hatred where Jews hardly exist). I believe in a separate, similar nation-state for the badly aggrieved Palestinian Arabs. They need one too, many Israeli and Diaspora Jews agree. But my subject here is a Diasporic Vision, Jewish and not; Diasporist painting of all things.

I don't wish to stray from the embarrassing focus of this little book, the recurrent theme of this period in my life – Jews

Yona in Paris 1982

in Peril, and my own ambiguous perception of peril in some of my pictures. Many of you will agree with me that we learn about life and its events by discovering or uncovering ourselves. Beyond that, or during that discovery, lies art in all its dramatic, controversial and depressing ambiguity. I'd like to call it art-time, the way scientists speak of space-time. The timeless Beckett may be paraphrased: (Art), that double-headed monster of damnation and salvation. At odd moments I even suspect art can mend the world a little. No, I'm certain it can because I have the experience of its company – the healing effect of its company, just the two of us like pals alone in a room together. Many will agree with the feeling.

The Secret Jew (First State) 1976

MANIFESTO

Kennst Du das Land? 1962 (detail)

Diasporist painting, which I just made up, is enacted under peculiar historical and personal freedoms, stresses, dislocation, rupture and momentum. The Diasporist lives and paints in two or more societies at once. Diasporism, as I wish to write about it, is as old as the hills (or caves) but new enough to react to today's newspaper or last week's aesthetic musing or tomorrow's terror. I don't know if people will liken it to a School of painting or attribute certain characteristics or even Style to it. Many will oppose the very idea, and that is the way of the world.

My embarrassment at pressing upon my dubious pictures and upon you the case of the Jews, against the advice of wiser heads, begins to feel less uncomfortable. It is, of course, a universal art, something which speaks to the world, to the common reader, which every painter desires, as religions and poetry wish to speak of and to our world. The world being what it is, like our art, it's a poor listener and it remains divided, but artists at least tend to gentler, less killing divisions. For a while, I will presume to bore you with pictures of an imperilled world

Germania (The Tunnel) 1985 (self-portrait detail)

you may know only as imperfectly as I do, if at all . . . or
I should say – pictures of part of my world just now. My
case is built on a cliché which may also be an insightful
art lesson. It is that the threatened condition of the Jews
witnesses the condition of our wider world. It is a radical witness. One hundred and fifty years ago, Heine
warned that where books were burned, human beings
would be. Keep in mind that art and life get quite
conjoined (art-time) in our modern tradition and sometimes blur. Later, when we are dead, the art is (life-less?)
alone in the room.

For the moment, Diasporism is my own School, neither particularly unhappy practice nor proud persuasion. I would
simply say it is an unsettled mode of art-life, performed
by a painter who feels out of place much of the time,
even when he is lucky enough to stay at work in his
room, unmolested through most of his days. His
Diasporism, to the extent that it marks his painting, re-
lies on a mind-set which is often occupied with vagaries
of history, kin, homelands, the scattering of his people (if
he thinks he may have a people), and such stuff. Is that
not a general meaning of Diaspora? More particular
meanings may leave deeper marks or even scars on
painting. It's not for me to spell out the quite various
Diasporic conditions proliferating everywhere now, except to say that Jews do not own Diaspora; they are not
the only Diasporists by a long shot. They are merely
mine. As if they were not in enough trouble right now,
as usual, the Israel-Diaspora problem is as difficult to
contemplate as the more usual problem of Jewish survival itself. Keening to seismic readings now that Israel

Passion (1940–45) Girl/Plume 1985

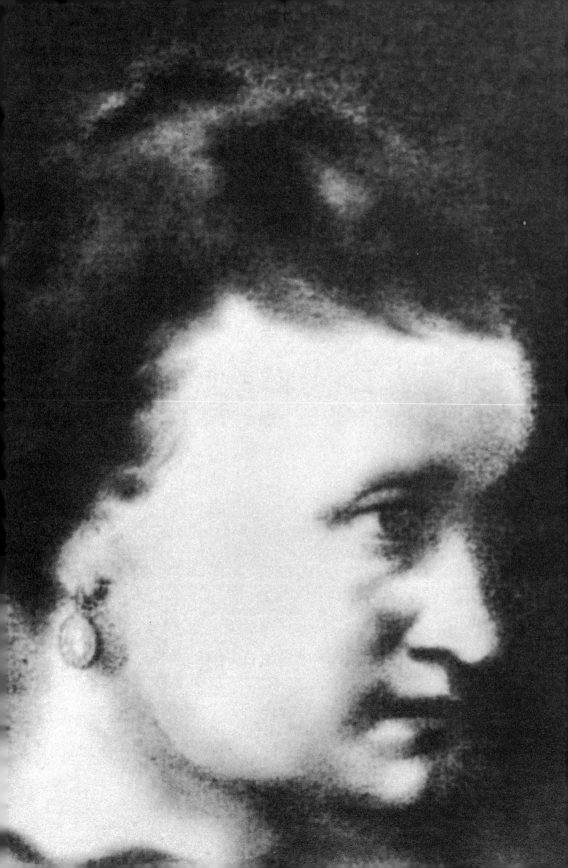

is reborn, the awful historical problem of Jewish political impotence is lessened, but I would greatly fear the consequences if most Jews were concentrated in the Holy Land, where it would be easier than ever to finish them off in a place the size of Greater Indianapolis, with a bomb or two! Being Jews though, there's energy enough left over, while enduring siege by a billion enemies, to argue the very finest points among ourselves concerning the question of Diaspora – not uninteresting arguments you can look up yourself, which I won't rehearse here except to say that the Jewish problem, which never seems to go away (*pace* George Eliot), gave birth, about a hundred years ago, to a serious Palestine-Diaspora equation which was to have delivered a 'normalcy' to the bloodied Jews and which now looks as elusive as the Messiah and the End of Days.

Since this is a manifesto, albeit not a very aggressive one (I haven't read Breton or Lewis or Marinetti and such since I was eighteen), I want it to be somewhat declarative because I think art and life are fairly married and I think I owe it to my pictures to put their stressful birth with some idiosyncratic precision.

What I owe to my pictures, I guess I owe to my readers, mostly to those few attentive or curious enough to interest themselves in the peculiar genesis of these disputed works I call Diasporist.

Like an aging bear, I am not often brave or cunning. I try to proceed from my cave with caution because I tend to blot my copybook, as the English say. Out I come at the

The Mother 1977 (detail)

wrong season, when the world is bemused daily by Jews
and their Holocausts, past and pending. As if that were
not enough, I just read in an art column that the time for
manifestos has passed. So I thought I'd write one, the
Belated Bear stumbling forward, brandishing his
paintbrush, into the tunnel at the end of the light. . . .

n my time, half the painters of the great Schools of Paris, New
York and London were not born in their host countries.
If there is nothing which people in dispersion share in
common, then my Diasporist tendency rests in my mind
only and maybe in my pictures . . . but consider: every
grain of common ground will firm the halting step of
people in dispersion as surely as every proof of welcome
has encouraged emigrés before in cosmopolitan centers.
Rootedness has played its intrinsic and subtle part in
the national art modes of Egypt, Japan, England, Holland
and the high Mediterranean cultures and city-states. I
want to suggest and manifest a commonality (for painting) in dispersion which has mainly been seen before
only in fixed places; but, not unlike painters who leave
those centers or those modes, such as Cézanne, who left
Paris behind for his epochal old-age style at home, or
Picasso who left (classical) Cubism in the lurch,
Diasporists also exchange their colors, for instance, to
the extent that they begin to really feel at home some-
where, or practice within a School, or indeed, refuse
what I say here. . . .

f a people is dispersed, hurt, hounded, uneasy, their pariah
condition confounds expectation in profound and complex ways. So it must be in aesthetic matters. Even if a

ighs from Hell 1979 (detail)

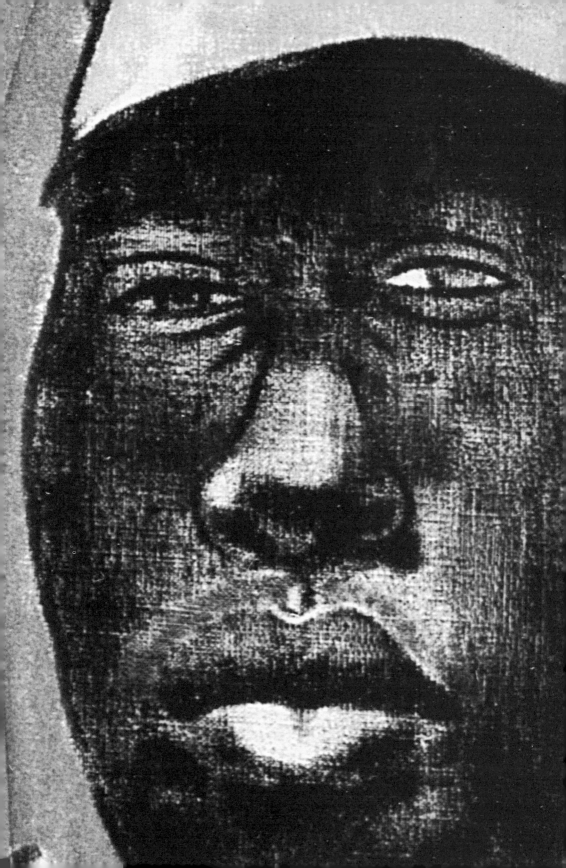

Diasporist seems to assimilate easily to prevailing aesthetics, as he does in most currents of life, the confound-
ing, uneasy side of his nature may also be addressed,
that deeper heart, as magical as anything the Surrealist
or Mystical-Abstractionist ever sought within himself. I
can only posit a new aesthetic for myself (to recreate myself) because I don't want to become a mouthpiece for
the traditions of general art, and because some things in
dispersion (ancient and modern) have come of age now
for me. As the quasi-Diasporist Gauguin said, 'I wish to
establish the right to dare anything.'

Aside from the always still endangered Jews (in a Masadic Israel and in Diaspora), there are other resounding
Diasporists – Palestinians prominent and suffering
among them. Israel Zangwill (1864–1926) placed the Ar-
menians at 'the pit of Hell', and in 1920 bowed before
their 'higher majesty of sorrow'. There is a Black African
Disapora as terrible and outstanding as any other, which
has disturbed my thoughts since early boyhood. Murderous Stalinism and Pol Potism must have all but unsung
Diaspora trails of their bloody own. What is left of these
dispersed peoples finds as little peace as Ahasuerus himself. If the art of these Diasporists, as they emerge from
historical fog, is not touched by their separate destinies,
God help them. He has so often not.

Like most human events, Diasporism is not clear-cut, hard or
fast (many movements in art are not), neither in its usual
and historic explications nor in the meanings I have be-
gun to feel for myself as a painter. As a Diasporist
painter, like the Realist, the Cubist, the Expressionist

ian de la Cruz 1967 (detail)

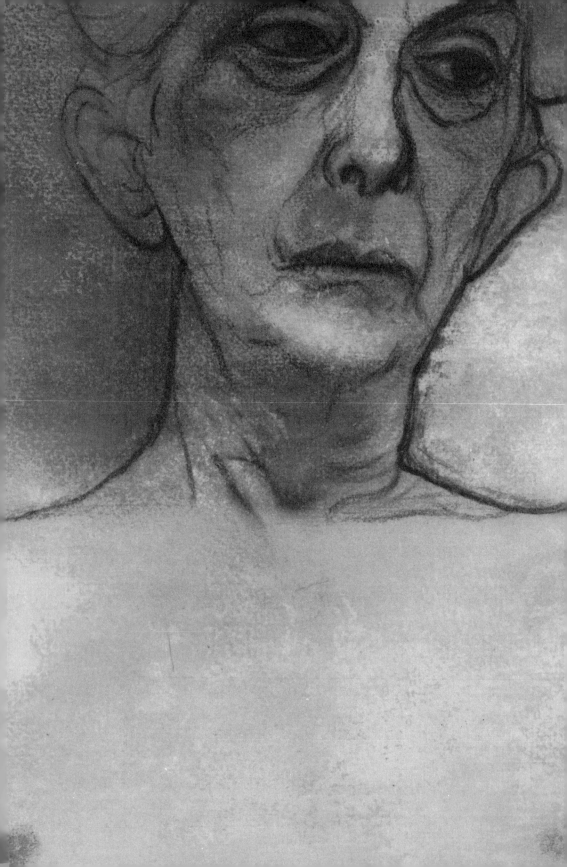

and other painters, I would resist exacting codification (rightly). Nor can I speak cogently for even more complex and speculative realms of the painter's make-up, for 'internal exile', the condition of the self-estranged sexual Diaspora and such. The Diasporist appears among emigrés and refugees, among the heirs of Surrealism, Naturalism, Symbolism and other aesthetics, among the home-grown, among nationalists and internationalists, pariahs and patriots, in every polyglot matrix, among the political and religious as well as those who do without politics and religion or are uncertain. *In the end, the Diasporist knows he is one*, even though he may one day settle down and sort of cease to be one. Many do not settle and that is a crux which will affect and, I think, effect the art. If human instincts for kin and home are primordial, as they so often seem, the Diasporic condition presents itself as yet another theater in which human, artistic instinct comes into play, maybe not primordial (?) but a condition, a theater to be treasured. As I write these words, I also know that if Diasporists become treasured, their theater will close, and open under a new sign and name, maybe with a curse upon it.

Diasporism is my mode. It is the way I do my pictures. If they mirror my life, these pictures betray confounded patterns. I make this painting mode up as I go along because it seems more and more natural for me, so natural that I think I've been a Diasporist painter from the start without knowing and then slowly learnt it in a twilit period, until it began to dawn on me that I should act upon it. Diasporist painting is unfolding commentary on its life-source, the contemplation of a transience, a

Quentin 1979 (detail)

Midrash (exposition, exegesis of non-literal meaning) in paint and somehow, collected, these paintings, these circumstantial allusions, form themselves into secular *Responsa* or reactions to one's transient restlessness, un-at-homeness, groundlessness. Because it is art of some kind, the act (of painting) need not be an unhappy one. Although my Diasporist painting grows out of art, as for instance, Cubism or Surrealism did, it owes its greatest debt to the terms and passions of my own life and growing sense of myself as a Diasporist Jew. I have spent half my life away from my American homeland, that most special Diaspora Jews have ever known. Until now, I've only rarely painted there and I set down these first exilic ruminations still from a bittersweet abroad, but written in my homesick, Americanist tense, haunted by the music of Diaspora.

I've always been a Diasporist Jew, but as a young man I was not sure what a Jew was. I was unaware that such questions were debated within Jewry, even in the Knesset itself. Jews were Believers, I thought, and I assumed you were whatever you believed in, that if you became a Catholic or an atheist or a Socialist, that's what you were. Art itself was a church, a universalist edifice, an amazing sanctuary from the claims and decrepitude of modern life, where you could abandon self and marry painting. My friend Isaiah Berlin says: 'A Jew is a Jew like a table is a table.' Now, that interests me greatly, but the thing was blurred in my youth. This was, I learned later, a classic assimilationist pose. My maternal grandfather had been a Socialist Bundist in Russia, on the run from the Czarist police. He passed on his reli-

Kitaj as a student in Vienna, 1950

gious skepticism to my mother, who brought me up as a freethinker with no Jewish education. Ours was a household full of secular Diasporists who seemed to be Jews only by the way. It would be many more years before I learned that the Germans and Austrians who did what they did in that time, when I was playing baseball and cruising girls, made no distinctions between Believers or atheists or the one and a half million Jewish infants who had not yet decided what they were when they got sent up in smoke. One third of all Jews on earth were murdered in my youth. It is well known that a Silence fell upon our world for some years after what Winston Churchill called 'probably the greatest and most horrible crime ever committed in the whole history of the world'. It was *the* break with traditional evil, its own archetype, someone said. The classic texts on the Holocaust are fairly recent and as I got around to them and the paradox of Jewishness began to enthrall me, the Diasporist painter in me started to grow alert, after a numbing, morbid period. The mystery of dispersion now seems to me as *real* as any located School known to art. I didn't know it at first, but I had stumbled upon a tremendous lesson, taught long ago by many conflicting personalities both Jewish and Gentile (Sartre, etc.), by such absorbing figures as Ahad Ha'am (1856–1927), that it is Jewishness that condemns one, not the Jewish religion. It became reasonable to suppose that Jewishness, this complex of qualities, would be a presence in art as it is in life. In Diaspora, life has a force of its own. So would Diasporist painting, never before particularly associated with pariah peoples. For me, its time has come at last.

Germania (The Tunnel) 1985 (detail)

Diaspora (dispersion in Greek) is most often associated with
      Jews and their two thousand-year old scattering among
      the nations (longer by other accounts). What the Jews
      call *Galut* (Exile in Hebrew), had become a way of life
      (and death), consonant with Jewishness itself, even
      though Israel is reborn. I am one of those who are pos-
      sessed by the consonance of art and life. Some are not. I
      think that memories, events and beliefs are sacred
      dreams for painting and so the mode of my life is trans-
      lated into pictures. In translation there is not ultimate
      accuracy, only an illusion of truth, as in art. Because nei-
      ther Diaspora nor Israel can live really happily ever after
      anyway (or so it increasingly seems) and a normative co-
      existence replaces the 'normalcy' once wished upon the
      state, many of us who make our lives in dispersion fol-
      low *its* peculiar, various, often very homelike (America),
      very complex destinies where, as someone put it, Jews
      have achieved emancipation without auto-emancipation.
      The compelling destiny of dispersion is one's own and
      describes my Diasporism, which describes and explains
      my parable-pictures, their dissolutions, repressions, asso-
      ciations, referrals and sometime difficulty, their text-ob-
      sessions, their play of differences, their autobiographical
      heresies, their skeptical dispositions, their assimilationist
      modernisms, fragmentation and confusions, their secular
      blasphemies, their longing allegiance to the exact art-
      past which corresponds to the historical moments when
      Jews became free to pursue a life in art (I mean from the
      late nineteenth century on).

Diasporist art is contradictory at its heart, being both
      internationalist and particularist. It can be inconsistent,

Michael Hamburger 1974

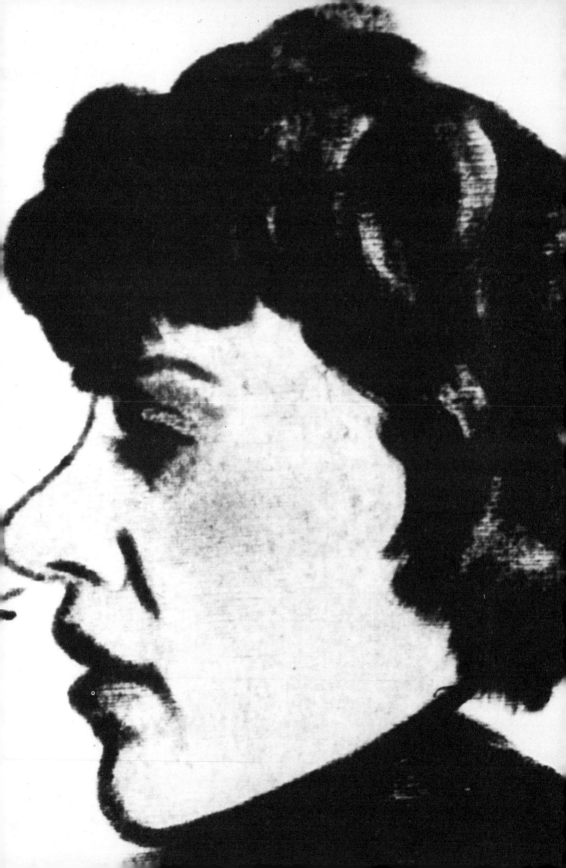

which is a major blasphemy against the logic of much art education, because life in Diaspora is often inconsistent and tense; schismatic contradiction animates each day. To be consistent can mean the painter is settled and at home. All this begins to define the painting mode I call Diasporism. People are always saying the meanings in my pictures refuse to be fixed, to be settled, to be stable: *that's* Diasporism, which welcomes interesting, creative misreading; the Zohar says that the meaning of the book changes from year to year! And now as I come to life again after fifty, the room in which I paint becomes a sort of permissive *cheder* (room, the room or school where one studies) in which art becomes what I *think*, dramatizing my mind's life, while the ancient religion itself whispers its Covenantal, mythic, Midrashic, ethical, exegetical, schismatic, Zaddik-ridden, arguments. There is a traditional notion that the divine presence itself is in the Diaspora, and, over one shoulder, *Sefirot* (divine emanations and 'intelligences' according to Kabbalah) flash and ignite the canvas towards which I lean in my orthopedic back-chair, while from my subconscious, from what can be summoned up from mind and nerve, and even after nature, other voices speak more loudly than the divines, in tongues learned in our wide Diaspora. These are the voices I mostly cleave to. Listen to them. They will tell you what a Diasporist has on his mind (Michelangelo said you paint with your mind) as he strokes his canvas.

he voices speak nervously about things unheard in painting
(or long forgotten) – of *ethnie*, of historical memories and
cultures, of ancestry myths and of heroes. Abraham's

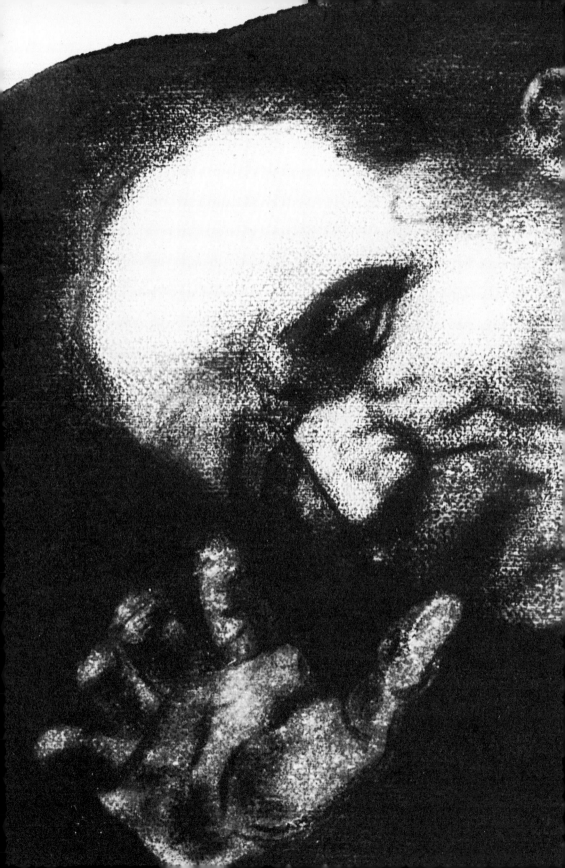

journey from Ur becomes, in the name of 'good' picturemaking (at my own easel), Joe Singer's secret lives, es-
capes, deaths and resurrections, reconstructed from
Diasporic myths which began when I did in 1932 and
will die with me – or live on, as for instance Daumier's
Ratapoil has, as Cézanne's mountain has. Those art mod-
els were not only radical patterns representing spatial
enquiry (which they also are) but profound *ethnie* (belonging to Paris, Provence, shared history). Yes,
Cézanne's mountain represents shared *tribal* (French)
history – the history of a bitter old Provençal genius
wrestling with his art angel on his own sacred southern
ground. That's what I want to be, a tribal remembrancer,
wrestling with my Diasporic angel; I feel a great affection
for this emancipating muse wherever I am at my painting. She is my favorite model. She suggests my frail en-
titlements and shaky destinies and let's-pretend art
aspirations.

One of the most recent of my hundred negative critics wrote in
his review of my 1986 exhibition that it was 'littered
with ideas'. Heavens to Betsy, I hope that's true. My poor
Diasporist mind urges me to wander among ideas without rest, always the false-scholar, which is often how we
painters make our mark. The pursuit of ideas, both religious and secular, at any cost, is often attributed to Jews
by both well-wishers and doubters. Hitler is said to have
accused the Jews of inventing conscience. Ideas and
painting are inseparable. The Diasporist pursuit of a
homeless logic of *ethnie* may be the radical (root) core of
a newer art than we can yet imagine . . . those of us who
think we can relate our past experience of Diaspora to a

he Listener (Joe Singer in Hiding) 1980 (detail)

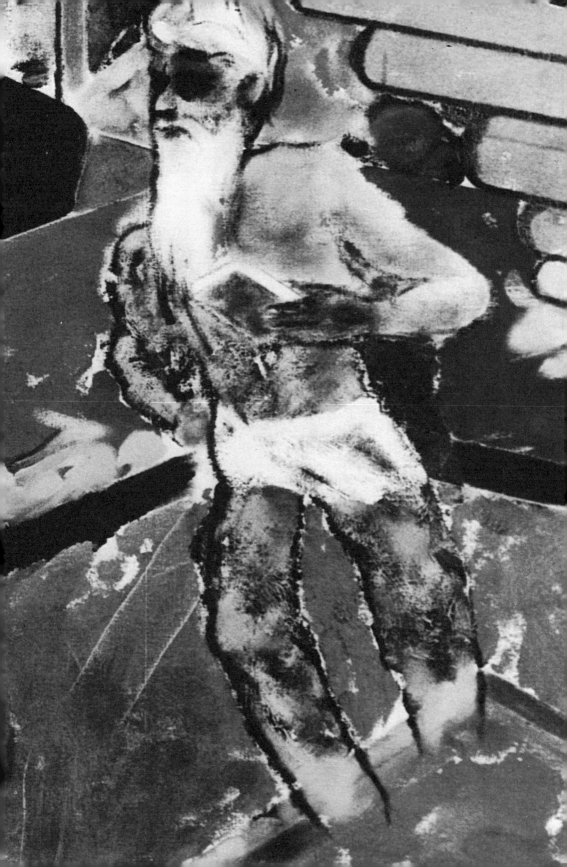

present understanding of it in painted, hopefully universal, pictures which may speak to many people.

Speaking of homeless logic, I must declare or confess my most complex credential – one of the outstanding facts of my life and Diasporic condition: utterly American, longingly Jewish, School of London, I spin my years away from both my heartlands, up to now anyway (age fifty-four). I suppose a case could be made for a Jewish heartland of the mind (the case of this text in fact), rather than Jerusalem or even New York. But the Americanist credential has another pedigree, surely touched upon by James, Cassatt, Sargent, Pound, Whistler, Epstein, Eliot, Stein and all my other forebears. Joyce and Lawrence were early hero-exemplars (art and life) and must have suffered/enjoyed a same confusion, but it is not my intention to drag all that expatriate weight across my present Diasporist musing and open up the membership. What did Groucho say? Something like he wouldn't want to join a club that would let people like him in?

In one of its self-definitions, Diasporism, *my* sort of Diasporism, has been lived and acted out in the free, Western, privileged, uninhibited, uncensored, permissive, élitist cloud-cuckoo lands of Modernism. Diasporism in art has been largely Assimilationist and Modernist, played on a diffuse stage with few constraints. Assimilationism is the prevailing mode in the art of our time. Young people are taught that they must strike chords which agree with *art* ('advanced' or not) without much regard to origin, milieu or creed – and so they may in our very few democracies. My own Diasporist mode resists (gently) the absolute

London, England, aged Self-Portrait 1982 (detail)

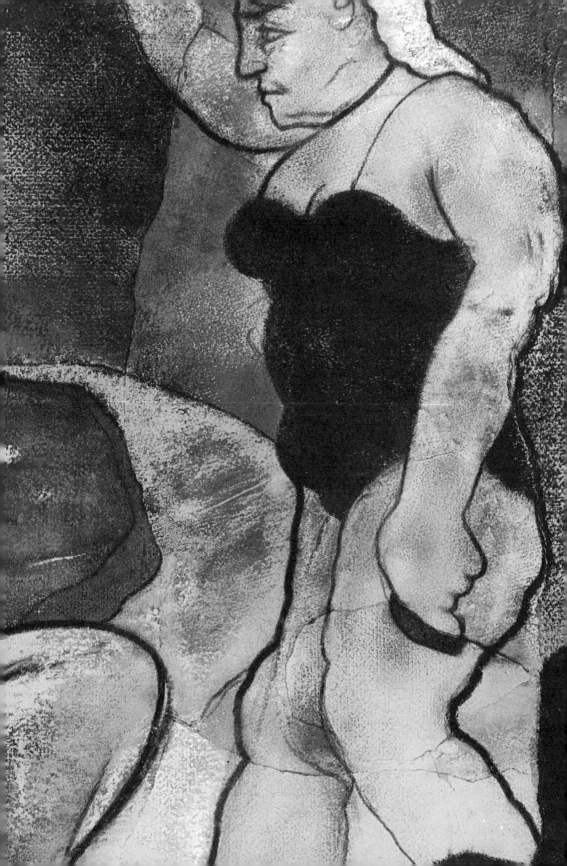

wisdom of assimilationism in art. I would rather find the energy to do for Jews at least what Morandi did for jars. Then I could take summers off like he did and paint landscapes or something. The Diasporist in me would deny neither painting, as it asks to be continued, nor the themes and obsessions which quicken my mind and heart. Looking back before my own time, I'd like to identify a First *Aliyah* (ascent) in Diasporic painting, which, in *its* time, accorded with a faith in Modernism and which was assimilated to it more than to any idea of one's origins. These Diasporists, aside from those Jews who ascended to Paris, may include honorary Jews like Mondrian, Picasso, Beckmann, Hofmann, the Surrealists and the Bauhaus people, many of whom escaped the Enemy of the Jews, often to find refuge among Diasporist Jews themselves, especially in New York. Painters like Picasso, Bonnard, Matisse and Munch who did not have to flee, were touched and encouraged throughout their lives by what may even be called a (Jewish) Diasporist aura of friends, collectors, dealers, writers, audience, explainers and colleagues, some of whom were to go up the chimneys (another ascent in Diasporist destiny). Although Diasporism in refugee Gentiles may be my own speculative construct, it is very real for Jews.

And what is real for Jews is real for Jewish painters. I suspect that even those who go out of their way to isolate art from the imagined merits or demerits of being Jewish are, in the very doing, anointing art with the troubled wand of Jewish Diasporism. To my mind, something instinct with one's culture enters into one's art. And so the lost and soon to be murdered world of East European Jewry

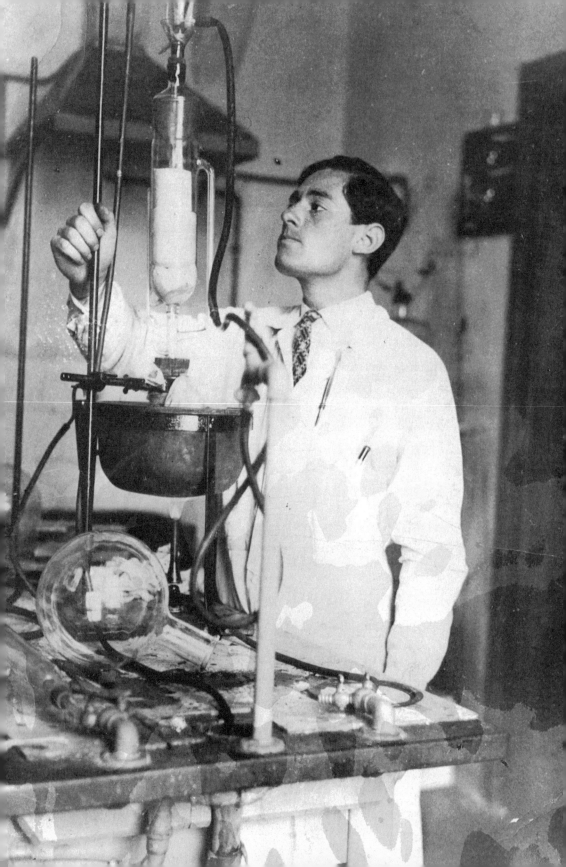

cultured the art of many Jewish painters, even as they assimilated to the powerful charms of the new Modernism. We know that from the School of Montparnasse. These early modern Diasporists lived and worked outside my own experience. The Kingdom of Death they left in the Pale, and the bittersweet Paris of their brief freedom is not for me to reconstruct. Nor is the amazing American sanctuary from 1900 to the present moment, where Diasporism achieved its Golden Age according to many people, and Diasporist painting reached its *second* modern coming (in my little history lesson). Before 1900 doesn't concern me here because Jews were only just preparing to arise from a Diasporic sleep of dreams and one third of them would (in the last days of humanity) unknowingly sleepwalk into an oven. After 1900 begins to touch my own pictures, first of all because my Yiddish- and Russian-speaking grandparents fled to America. So did my father. Then, after the Anschluss, so did my stepfather Kitaj and, after the war, my grandmother Kitaj. I am not only a Diasporist but a Biographical Heretic, among other things, and so I have a peculiar faith and interest in the influence not only of past art acting on one's pictures – everyone agrees about that – but also of one's youth, upbringing, friends, milieux. Can anyone doubt that we are fatally rooted in the first part of our life? I am given to my time in art as any painter is. It *tells* in our pictures. Our pictures speak our particular culture and the languages of general as well as tribal cultures which interest us most. That picture-speech is uttered through personality, which is something perceived in its very achievement, like all cultural stuff. I'm not content that the vivid marriage of forms and contents

Dr Walter Kitaj as a student
at the University of Vienna, 1937?

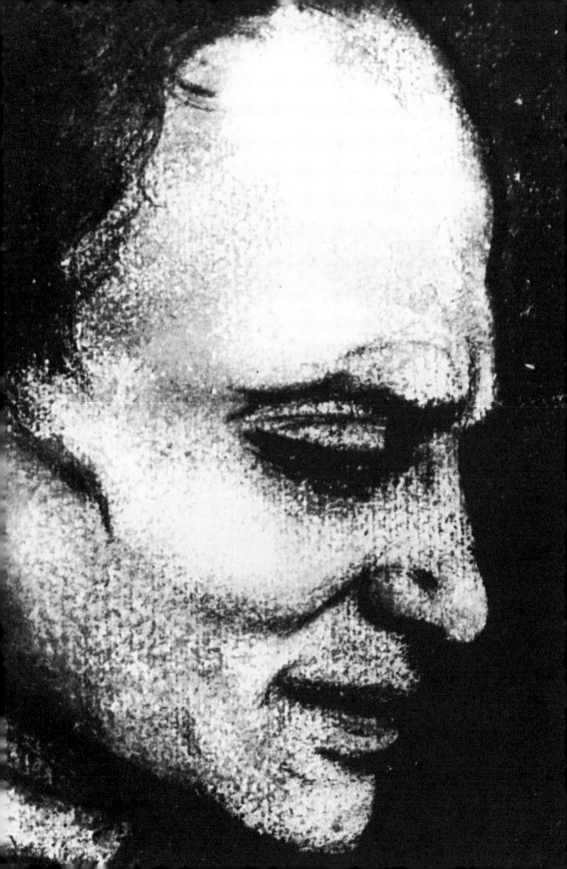

in painting be known aside from our particular, even singular cultures and predicaments. I like to think this cultural marriage drama may be seen to be done up in pictures. Picasso said it: 'It is not sufficient to know an artist's works. It is also necessary to know when he did them, why, how, under what circumstances.'

Post-Holocaust Diasporism then. I can't speak for the Jews or Gentiles of the Abstract School of New York and their explainers, Diasporists though many were, except to express a hunch that they kept to only *some* avenues of their creativity, large scale though it was, nor for any of my comrades in what I have called (in *The Human Clay*, 1976) the School of London, some of whom are Diaspora Jews and some of whom may wander in a sexual Diaspora. I will only say there is no doubt in my mind that this Second Diasporic Aliyah (pray God will forgive me this impertinent usage), roughly from Rothko to Auerbach, has been touched by its destiny, a destiny which is *driven* and driven to remember (like some great art before), the worst thing imaginable.

Diasporism didn't exist in painting until I invented it, but it has antecedents, like Surrealism had in Dada and Symbolism, and Abstractionism had in, say, theosophy and ornament. Since we artists tend to create our precursors, as Borges said, Diasporist painting now, for me, began in the great art of the West which nourishes all painters, including those of the briefly fluttering congeries of modernist styles, Yiddishkeit and doomed café freedoms which ended at Drancy and the Eastern railheads. Using the Hebrew term, the present Pope, John Paul II, just

Two London Painters: Frank Auerbach 1979 (detail).
Los Angeles County Museum of Art (Blankfort donation)

said: 'This is *still* the century of the Shoah.' Indeed, my own Diasporism turns on my century still, both in the sense the Pope meant and, as a painter, in the cosmo-politan (and early Diasporist) moments in a modern art which was to live on and flourish, after Paris, mainly in the English-speaking world, my world. For the Diasporist Jew and Gentile (as for the Israeli) it is a world in the making and fraught with danger and mystery. For me, art is in the making in *that* world. Some years ago, I thought this might be a period I would pass through, but Diasporism, one's Jewishness itself, changes all the time. Any exciting life of the mind will keep changing one's art. The more I throw in my lot with the Jewish destiny or cultural tribe or nation or whatever it is, and the closer I get to my own death, the more a vision of Diasporic art draws me forward.

If any curious people have followed this stuff of mine thus far, my gentle manifesto is also a primitive and belated answer to those who have written to me during recent years asking for advice I could only rarely give. I don't want to enlist them as Diasporists – Jewish or otherwise. My tendency is to throw these few crumbs down at the feet of our modern art and run like hell into hiding.

Self-Portrait as a Woman 1984 (detail)

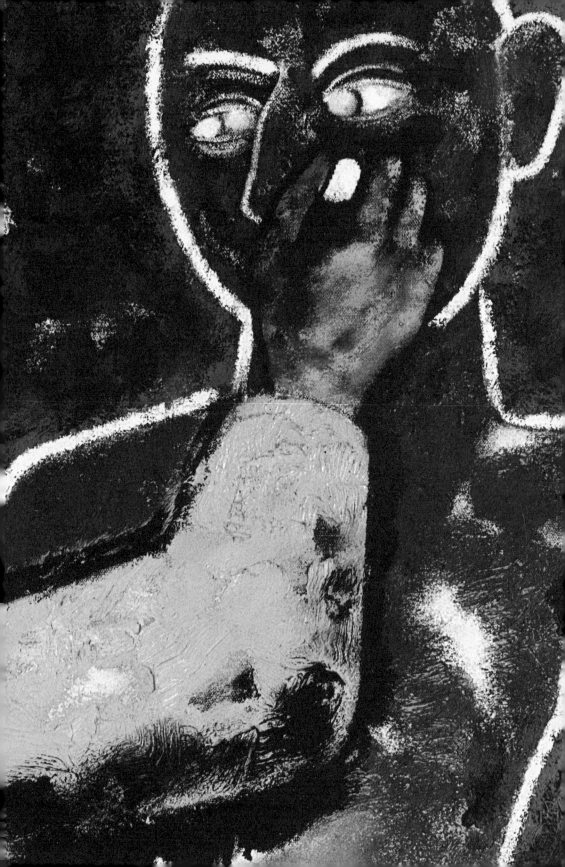

HOW I CAME TO MAKE MY DIASPORIST PICTURES (UNTIMELY THOUGHTS)

I have always been meaning to explain the way in which I came to write certain books.

It involved a very special method. And it seems to me that it is my duty to reveal this method, since I have the feeling that future writers may perhaps be able to exploit it fruitfully.

Raymond Roussel

The Jewish School (Drawing a Golem) 1980 (detail)

After almost a lifetime as a painter, my painting thoughts begin
　　　to dwell on whether or not the Jews are a nation, or a
　　　state of mind, or what they are; among the answers lies
　　　an aesthetic, I sometimes think, which drives me in style
　　　and uncertainty toward that shore. Many, but not all, of
　　　my recent pictures and good intentions are stacked in
　　　that leaking rowboat whose oars I pull excitedly, fearful
　　　of sinking in unknown waters.
　　　■

In the Diaspora I have known, one is free to dare anything; in
　　　many other places one can't. The idea of a 'safe' *Galut*
　　　milieu may prove yet again to be an illusion: the
　　　Diasporist as daring Illusionist. Let it tell in the picture,
　　　that magic trick.
　　　■

The Diasporist, like other painters, can persist in intention, in
　　　aspiring to characteristic style to the point of surprise.
　　　Others will succeed where I may fail because, however
　　　characteristic, a Diasporist manner or figure of thought

Gestapo prison, Warsaw, 1972 (photo by Kitaj)

(in art) feels very exposed, primitive in a sense new to art; still in the most dread century for the Diasporist to come of age, after all.

■

Forever and a day, and long after Adorno (1903–69), people will argue about whether or not 'art' can or should touch upon the Shoah. The fact is that no one can touch anything but its shadow, which lies across the paths of some of us, however indistinct. Like most people, I only know the shadow, its aspect in my life. No one has cogently attacked me yet for the ways the shadow has affected my pictures – that will come; but so far there's been only a little faint grumbling here and there and a bit of concerned head-shaking. In the lives of those who were *there*, the shadows, *their* shadows are not indistinct at all. They are called *memories*. It feels very strange/awful/awe-full to be alive, still, in the stinking aftermath of the Shoah, to know people who were *there* during that time. Giotto and Michelangelo and Rembrandt knew *their* Passion, its central locus in their lives, more than a thousand years after the event. In the studio, what can be said? What can be faced? I think I know (for the moment). It is what the splendid R. P. Blackmur (1904–65) called 'the radical imperfection of the intellect striking on the radical imperfection of the imagination'.

■

Israel is a land the Jews found again (after two thousand years) at great cost to themselves and to other people. Like many Diasporists (who don't live there), I fear for its pre-

The Painter (Cross and Chimney) 1984–85
(detail after Giotto)

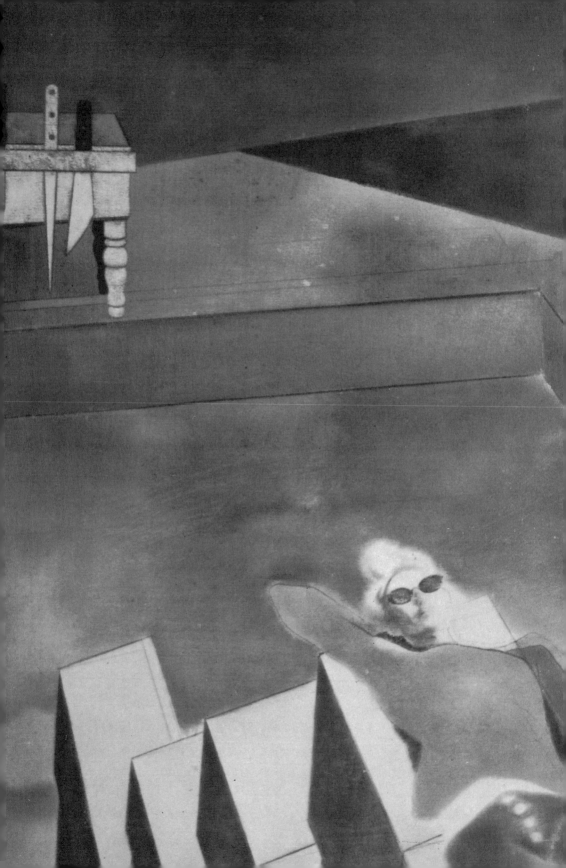

carious, self-emancipated life, *and* the lives of the Arab
Diaspora. What cost Diaspora? Diasporist painting will
be valued, despised and endangered according to either
its own rules or, as usual, to host rules (and sufferances),
host threats. In other words, the Diasporist painter might
as well make up his painting mode as he goes along and
not depend too much on what the Romans do. That's
how I try to get through each painting day now. It's
called Auto-Emancipation in an important pamphlet by
Leo Pinsker (1821–91), which can be taken as a docu-
ment of a modern art, as I do. Sometimes I think upon its
terms while I paint, the way some painters listen to a
piece of music.

I begin now, in the beautiful London spring of 1987 to believe
that the meanings of paintings are inexhaustible. Paintings can't mean *only* what I say or suggest they do any
more than people can be depended upon for their absolute verification of intent, for flawless mastery of themselves and their acts. I don't wish to chew over what is
best left to philosophers. I would only defend (as I
always have) the personality, and thus the humanity,
which informs line, stroke, touch and *idea* in the painting art, against finality of assertion, interpretation (and
even execution) – but in *this* new way, in dispersion,
who shall decide what a painting means? My hosts?
Brother Diasporists, wrapped in their own enigmas? My
own exegeses are only more self-centred . . . under-
written by me, the Midrashist you can trust; my explications and the works themselves destabilize perfectability,
not to ruin it, but to enhance the 'affectionate intimacy'*

Malta 1974 (detail)

*I owe this term to Robert Alter.

in which the painting was born. Pictures will be 'better' for it, less 'successful' in their variant achievements, failures and readings run through the hands of a subversive Jew.

■

Almost thirty years ago, under the spell of Diasporists like Aby Warburg, Fritz Saxl, Edgar Wind and the Surrealists, I made a little painting called *His Cult of the Fragment*. I was a fragmented cultist ten years before I discovered Walter Benjamin (1892–1940), the exemplary and perhaps ultimate Diasporist and *his* cult of the fragment. It would be fifteen years before I ever heard the term Midrash and became transfixed by the artful and highly Diasporist history of that very real exegetical tradition within Jewish history. Thirty years later, I've learned of the Diasporists of the Ecole de Yale and their crazed and fascinating Cult of the Fragment (based on their French Diasporist mentor). Things sure do Only Connect. I'm just a poor struggling painter. Like most painters I have very little time left over to study the extra-painting profundity of these comrade Diasporists but, at my own sweet pace, I try; they make me a little crazier day by day. They encourage me in my old rowboat full of unfinishable canvases, some plain-spun, others too difficult, as many say of me.

■

If I say 'Jewish Art' to people, even to dear friends, Jewish or not, it's like saying 'the world is round' in 1491. Each new painting sails off where there be monsters.

■

The Jew, Etc. 1976–79 (detail)

A Diasporic nation feels half-lost, part hidden, much exposed
(Pinsker called the Jewish nation ghost-like). Painting appears to me a hidden act, secretive, then suddenly exposed, shown off to the world. Like the repository
findings in the Genizah at Cairo, one's pictures, one's
most secret findings, seek refuge but become crazily des-
tined for show. As I play out my life I would slow down
that dangerous public side because I prefer to reveal the
art to myself, more slowly in the doing . . . slow,
Midrashic paintings about the damned life; quicker,
nervy Jewish drawings and sketches made on the run, as
a man grows older, preserving secrets for better times.
■

There are no traditional Diasporist procedures (traits there may
be), so I like to improvise from picture to picture, learning as I go, like an itinerant pedlar or a fresh Harvard
boy or a whore's client or a little kid with fleas or a good
husband. Pictures can be made to agree with and surprise events, intentions and fantasies: the Diasporist as
Assimilationist Pariah Improvisationist.
■

Ill and good winds blow through Diaspora and breathe on the
Diasporist's artistic upbringing. I always know I may
have to move on, to get out before it's too late, and so I
daydream about other places while I'm painting. One
dream leads to another and changes the aspect and di-
rection of the picture if exilic longing moves the brush
from beyond. Quite a few paintings get made like that:
would-be Refugee Diasporist pictures.
■

Kenneth Anger and Michael Powell 1973 (detail).
Museum Ludwig, Cologne

There are very real shifts of received meaning among the audience of even the most sophisticated painting, even from beholder to beholder. Meanings in my own pictures change over the years, like the way you understand your child during certain years, and then you both grow older and you mean different things to each other. There is a human impulse to resolve ambiguity. The painting, like the child (or parent) may very well resist harmony and pattern. I believe that Diasporist painting shows its uneasy origins most tellingly in its most irreconcilable positions, in its very human discords. The Jewish traditions of Midrashic and Talmudic enquiry thrive on difficulties, as everyone knows. Men of Spirit wrote the Bible and Men of Spirit sometimes paint great pictures which will not and need not unravel (not even Mondrian). In painting as in parenting, you can't stack the cards anticipating final answers. In exegesis from the time of Akiva (c. 50–c. 132), indeterminacy of meaning is quite compatible with truth and meaning. I believe Cézanne, Cubism, Picassoism, Abstractionism and Diasporism share aspects of indeterminacy.

■

If it's true that the Diasporist doesn't 'belong' – and I don't know whether it is – Diasporist painting may be an art of failed monuments to a tradition without many traditions. Who will want to preserve these pictures? Where will they be buried, these strange notations the painter returns to each day and tries on like refugee shoes? Unless the Diasporist does belong, and truly nourishes national arts.

■

Painting 1983–85 (detail)

I paint pictures in a Diasporist mode possible only now, after
all that's happened and before all that may happen. That
could be why it's appropriate that I'm so disliked by
those who think I've bitten off more than I can chew. I
intend to keep chewing all the new food that didn't exist
for me when I was a young painter.

The Diasporist in me is impatient with host-art. I feel like a
guest in the house of art, guilty if I don't perform up to
snuff, anxious to leave the table (and table talk) as early
and politely as I can. That's really how I make my pictures, Diasporist pictures – feigned *politesse*, anxious resolve barely revealed. The older I get, closer to the end, I
look to more candid, x-rated designs upon painting.

After black slavery (its trail still unwinding), and this totalitar-
ian century (not yet done), it is the very frailty of the
human enterprise and the pathos, as an example, of
painting quietly through one's days, which assume
resonances, some of which I can state unequivocally: I
would urge Diasporist painting to a less frail passage, as
it tries to read and translate those forces which would
deny it life. In this respect, I try to be, along with many
artists, forward-looking – in fact, a Messianist.

For the Diasporist, art will turn on Passions never quite spent.
Painters and writers know well enough (or wish they
knew) how an art can unfold, for the first time, for the
only time perhaps, recent or distant histories, mysterious

4 *a.m.* 1985 (detail)

and removed witness and lost myth, as Michelangelo did on little sheets of paper and on vast ceilings, as the Bible does, as Tolstoy did about wars that were fought thirty years before he was born, as Proust and Picasso did around the crucial days of their lives. Even the instant an artist looks up from a drawing at its subject becomes dramatic history, after all.

■

Steering fitfully between European/American painting mores and traditionalist and modern Jewish obscurantism makes for exhilarating seamanship for me. Facing a canvas in that mood or upbringing is an exciting Diasporist freedom, to be cherished in each brush stroke – the briefly free, engaged Diasporist stroke, tempered like the Chinese or Japanese brush strokes, by very long history.

■

Anyone who reads fairly widely comes across the phrase 'the Jewish Question' over and over again. It occurs in many histories, among thinkers, in novels, in anti-Semitic writing, among the Zionist founding fathers and their opponents (Jewish and not), everywhere in my own experience. Sometimes it's called a 'problem'. Diasporist painting takes up this question or problem. Diasporist painting is problemic. Its very paint stirs up these questions and problems from a new painterly vantage, where each stroke is a benerved Diasporist signature.

■

In my journal, someone asks: is it not the duty of the Jew to be a difficult one, to himself first, and then to others, wher-

Erie Shore 1966 (detail). Nationalegalerie, Berlin, Staatliche Museen, Stiftung Preussischer Kulturbesitz

ever he may find himself? I don't know who wrote that, but when I'm sick of being difficult, I get a pencil and draw a friend. What if the friend is a Diasporist, as I am? What if I've just put aside a difficult Diasporist picture-composition, and will return to such a thing before long? The poor 'simple' drawing will become contaminated with difficulty – and it's not at all simple to draw a friend anyway.

Paintings sit there, looking out at the world, which remains separate. I'm for an art into which the painter imports things from the world that he cares about, passed rigorous art-customs officials unused to free entry of dissident baggage. Diasporist paintings come from afar but no one need fear them or what a critic called their 'close-knit' connections. They are sometimes interesting international treasures, even when they appear suspect or down-at-heel or embarrassing in their newly modern aura of group-self in what someone has called our *post* age.

Emil Fackenheim (b. 1916) believes the unresisting acceptance of *Galut* as meaningful is coming to an end (highly disputed). If Diaspora is fading away (I have no idea if it is or not), the idea of painting ridiculous pictures day after day, in dispersion, feels like the last days in a transit camp, with your thin mattress in a roll at the foot of the bed. I hardly buy brushes any more or clean the old ones well. They may just last me to their grubby end.

Arikha Sketching 1982

Very much out of context (but not out of mine), I want to grasp some words of the exalted Leo Baeck (1873–1956) from a fascinating paper by my friend and Baeck's student, Rabbi Daniel Silver. Baeck says: 'Every people can be chosen for a history, for a share in the history of humanity. Each is a question which God has asked, and each people must answer.' Hubris or not, I think each painter is also asked and, at my own peculiar Diasporic easel, aside from the (for me) overwhelming mystery of the absence or exit or (what?) of God in the Shoah, the *Where Was He?* – for the people who invented Him – I must answer many questions, such as: when I paint, how can I relate a past experience, even moments past, to a present understanding of it? What part is played by misunderstanding of history, long and recently past? Can't pictures also be prophetic; and falsely so?

■

Diasporist painting is the other side of the coin of Intimist painting. The coin itself is a Symbolist heir. The clever Intimist observes what he wants to see in his room, before the world outside his room begins; the Diasporist betrays art in his anxiety to depart from his lodgings or to return from the world.

■

You don't have to be a Jew to be a Diasporist; certainly not, but even when it comes to my own painting, my confidence wanes at its doorstep because the Jewish trail there, the Diasporic trail, leads through stylistic thickets and allegiance to historical painting ambitions which confound and, I hope, initiate forms of my own. If you make your

Kitaj and his daughter, Dominie, 1969? (photo by J.S.)

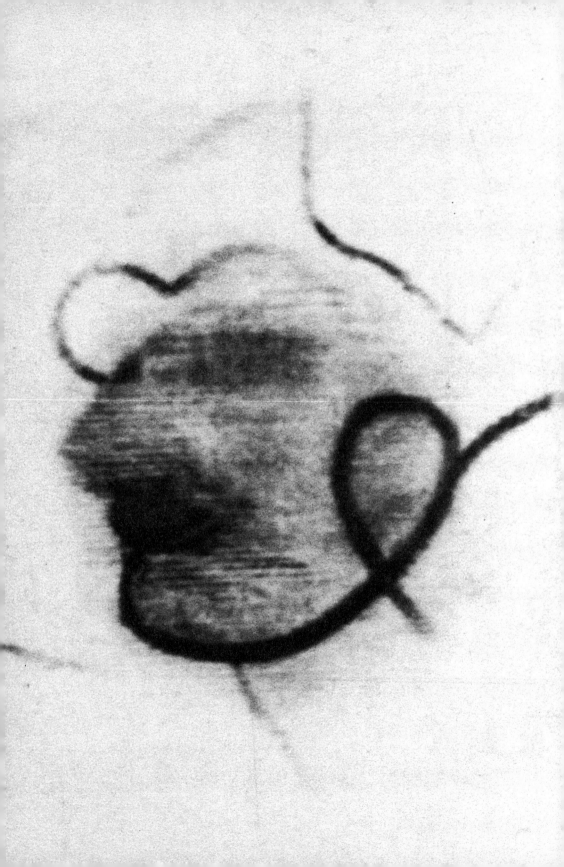

life in dispersion, you are never sure of the terms of
what makes you distinct enough to initiate anything. But
such 'doubt' is the very stuff of art: Cézanne, for instance, arguably an internal exile, was unwilling and unable not to irritate his art and his neighbors, like a Jew.
■

Concerning the Spiritual in Art (I've kept Kandinsky's book
since I was given it in teenage): the Jews have been
called a Spiritual nation – by Ahad Ha'am, by Simon
Dubnow (1860–1941), by many others – a people who
lived without a territory for two millennia, always ready
to move, as the Spirit moves. I don't know what they are
(and that excites *my* spirit) – nation or movable crowd or
race, people of the Book, sometimes not – but the Spiritual in art appeals to me and a Spiritual nation can belong to a Spiritual art; and even form one as rarely
before.
■

Diasporist history has its ups and downs. I suspect a *depressive*
connection which formulates its own aesthetic. Typical
figures here would be Primo Levi, Soutine, Kafka, Celan,
Bomberg, Benjamin, Jean Améry, Rothko, painters X, Y
and Z. . . . Diasporists who are not Jews will speak for
themselves.
■

As in Cubism, the Diasporist painting I have always done also
often represents more than one view. But I am mostly
drawn to variably modulated pictures of the mind at
work, instinctive *paint-dramas* of incertitude, views

wrapped around imagined themes and variations, the
contradictions of Diasporic life, apotheoses of groundlessness. I'm sorry and excited to be so difficult and
unpopular.
■

Diasporism has inspired those representations or fictions of
types of people to whose pictures I have given titles end-
ing in *ist* – Orientalist, Neocubist, Arabist, Remembrist,
Cézannist, Sensualist, Communist and Socialist,
Kabbalist, Caféist, Hispanist, and so on. I believe in a
type-coining power for art. Some have been friends; all
have been Diasporists (mostly not Jewish), folk who com-
plicate one's world in strange and wonderful ways.
These people have not taken Pascal's advice, which is
something like: all the trouble in the world is caused by
people who do not know how to stay in their own room.
I'm glad they didn't because their dispersed lives have
broken mediocre patterns and searched out cosmopolitan
treasure. Compliance with thug-mediocrity has bedeviled
our time. As Wiesel said, the 'Sheepishness' of the murdered was nothing compared to the sheep-like obedience
of their murderers. When you create a fiction or character in a picture, the character is pictured to be *seen*, dear
detractor, not 'literary' to be read (except in the mind's
eye?).
■

Diasporist painting, like the Diasporist, is a universal conun-
drum, a most ancient mystery presence, a secreted
reflection upon one's uneasy world. The Diasporist (Jew,
Black, Arab, Homosexual, Gypsy, Asian, emigrés from

The Arabist 1975–76 (detail).
Museum Boymans-van Beuningen, Rotterdam

despotism, bad luck, etc.) is widely despised, disliked, mistrusted, sometimes tolerated, even taken up here and there and shown a nice life. If a Jew gets himself to Israel, seemingly among his own, he often remains dislocated. He may not call himself Diasporist any more, but now he becomes Besieged (and a potential Diasporist). If I were a praying man, I would pray he does not become a Masadist. Diasporist painting is uneasy, alert, too well read in the ways of the world, but not well enough read in the ways of current aesthetics to satisfy schoolmen: it would be a deader duck than it is if it satisfied. You can never be sure how well assimilated the Diasporist painter is in the Man's country and so, as people do in ordinary life, the Diasporist does in our very extraordinary painting life. He blends and he does not; he breaks and trips over rules and molds assumed by the clairvoyants of assimilationist aesthetics. Jews and other Diasporists are noted irritants anyway (including many of these clairvoyants).

Simon Dubnow, the great old theoretician of Diaspora, thought that his dispersed and despised people would find peace in the various places where they settled among enlightened hosts. Then the Germans shot him. I don't know all his argument. I'm still studying it. Was there an awful constant he neglected in the life of nations? History makes it seem so. That fateful problem hangs over Diasporist painting like a roof that can cave in at any moment. How can it not affect the life of forms in one's picture of the world? And yet the received wisdoms the painter brings to his picture easily circumvent such

Sir Ernst Gombrich 1986. National Portrait Gallery, London

things, constant threat or not. It's not unusual even for
me to lose myself in 'pure' art. I hope Dubnow's dream
for Diaspora will come true. I also hope the paradise
in Zion and a longed-for Palestinian Arab national
homeland will both, and not at the cost of each other,
emerge and prosper under the sun. Then the *art* in
art may seem, for my dubious purposes anyway, to
resolve itself as Dubnow thought Diasporic polity would
in liberal societies. Don't hold your breath though!
I do not.

■

They must be doing something wrong, these Jews (and other
Diasporists). No one wants to be in trouble all the time. I
have decided that because of the trouble they are always
in, they are precious subjects for paintings. They should
be studied carefully, lovingly, instead of hated; and treasured in art rather than threatened. I'm told they are the
only people whose Golden Age lies in the future. The
monotheist God, Abraham, Moses, the Prophets, Maim-
onides, the Psalmist, Christ, Marx, Spinoza, Freud, Kafka
and Einstein all tell the future. They tell of promise. One
outcome of my study of this strange people of mine is
that painting, Diasporist painting in my own life, begins
to assume some of the Jewish attributes or characteristics assigned to that troubled people. The listing of traits
would be endless and funny. For the moment I will leave
all that to my buddy Philip Roth (b. 1933) and his great
book *The Counterlife*, which is quite encyclopedic on
these questions. I think that what the Jews promise,
paintings may be made to promise.

■

Arabs and Jews (The Dead Sea) 1970–86 (detail)

Nationalism seems awful; its track record stinks, but patriotism doesn't seem half bad. Love, or something like it, for people in trouble, coupled with love for your own troubled people is a stirring and complex mind-set for painting and its subjects. On the other hand, if people want their own homelands, why not? Partitioned homelands seem better to me than killing each other. My own homeland, America, and my little one, England, offer such strong *appearances* of peace and freedom that the really odd and peaceful practice of painting spins out my own Diasporic days and years until I can't sense any other way to go. The Diasporist at peace? His very presence among the nations is a rich and dangerous answer to the proposition that men are murderous.
■

There is nothing in Diasporism as a painting persuasion that has to interfere with good, surprising, unusual, life-enhancing, radical or not so radical picturemaking – any more than there is in Naturalism, Japanese art, Abstractionism and so on. The outcome will rise from the descent into Self and wander through all the World. The universalizing patterns and archetypes that always recur in much good painting are not ahistorical after all, and do not retain for each period or indeed for every frame of mind, changeless unities and meanings. For myself, I choose not to abandon myself to aestheticism in this climactic, restless age. Timeless archetypes are seductive creatures nevertheless and when I begin each painting day, I'm confronted with the question of subordinating detail of time and place, of re-inventing such things.
■

A Student of Vienna 1962

What does Diasporist painting look like? I think it looks like
my pictures. At first, Cubism only looked like the paintings of two painters; then four or five; then a few hundred. I will write about each of my pictures in some way
and in more or less detail because I'm a Village Ex-
plainer. These paintings are the 'proofs', examples and
failures of my Diasporist tendency. Meanwhile, this
manifesto is an affectionate shot across the bows of so
much received aesthetic opinion.

The Orientalist 1976–77 (detail).
The Trustees of the Tate Gallery, London

DIASPORIST
CITATIONS

However much the Jews adapted themselves, in language, manners, to a large extent even in the forms of religion, to the European peoples among whom they lived, the feeling of strangeness between them and their hosts never vanished. This is the ultimate cause of anti-Semitism, which cannot be got rid of by well meaning propaganda. Nationalities want to pursue their own goals, not to blend.

Albert Einstein

The Jewish School (Drawing a Golem) 1980 (detail)

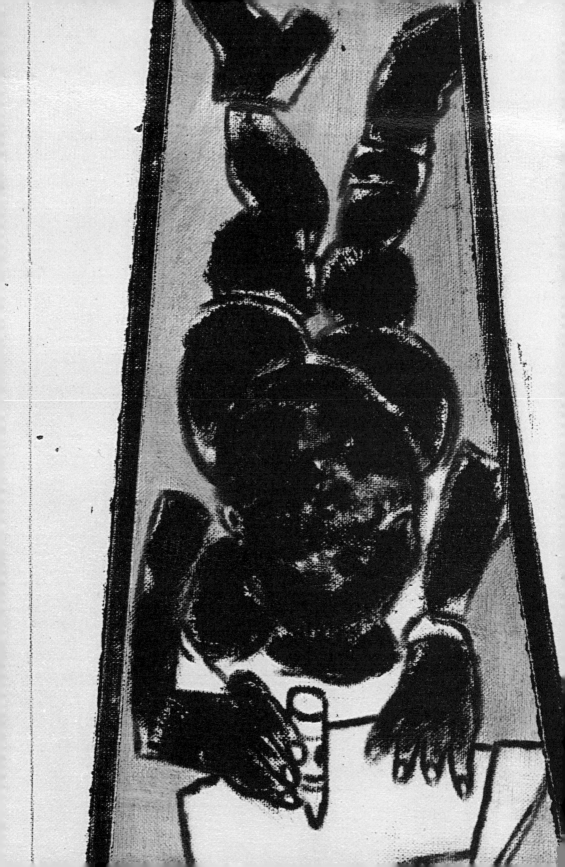

GUERNICA

Your place, young painter, is at the side of the people who defend freedom and, at the same time, the artistic and cultural patrimony of Spain.

Pablo Picasso

consider *Guernica* to be a Diasporist painting, at least as much as it is Cubist, Surrealist, Socialist/Antifascist, Picassoist. There was certainly a Spanish Diaspora during the fascist years. It was a Diasporist plight for a Spaniard to have camped across his border, by choice, destiny, anger, fear or expulsion, and to have artfully contrived, in the preeminent cosmopolitan milieu, an ultimate Diasporist synthesis. To my mind, the very deeply rooted Provençal Cézanne (and therefore a Diasporist no longer) had baked Impressionism into the final synthesis of his great southern bathing machines, to which Picasso replied as a young relocated Spaniard in the *Demoiselles d'Avignon*. Only later, when he couldn't or wouldn't return to Spain, I call him a Diasporist of a singular kind (which one hopes to be in any case).

HIS NEW FREEDOM

All insubstantial souls aspire to possess an identity of their own, and it is that identity that I seek in life and in my work.

Max Beckmann

Diasporist painters tend to be what used to be called 'emancipated' and therein lies a lot of delectable contradictions.
The Diasporist feels uneasy, alert to his new freedom,
groundless, even foreign – until or unless he feels very
much at home, and then he can hardly feel Diasporist
any more (until the next jolt). Meanwhile the Diasporist
pursues the phantom myths of nervous histories he
claims for his own, into the intractable swamps of ambiguous painting. The only place which seems less uncertain than the wide world is the room in which the
Diasporist tries out his pictures, which are about and decided by that Diasporic world outside his room (and the
bookish terrors and daydreams inside). But all good
painters must stay in their rooms. Nietzsche defines art,
beautifully I think, as the desire to be different, the de-

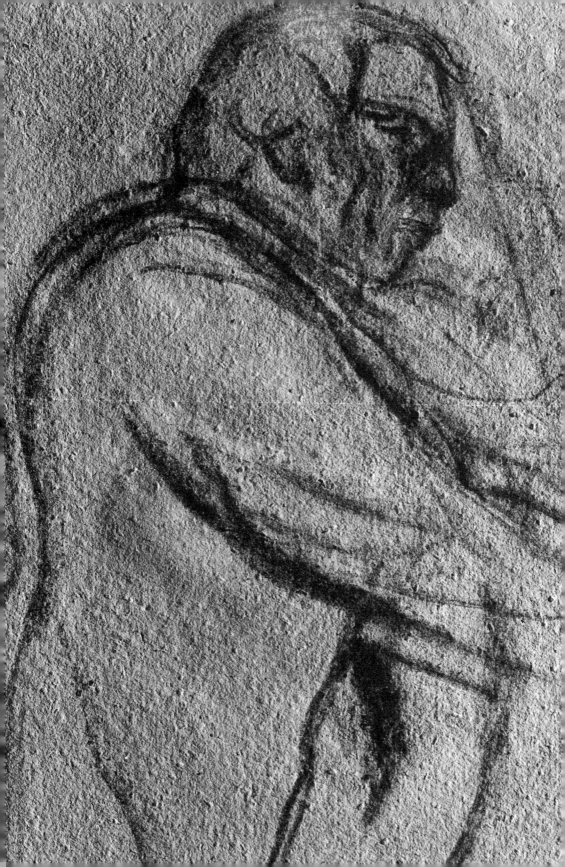

sire to be elsewhere. Painters are a herd of differing loners. So are Diasporists loners (and elsewhere too). The Jew in Europe in our time could not have been more alone, especially on his way to be murdered, among his people. They were destroyed as their emancipation had blossomed. Their greatest danger and their greatest freedom (their emancipated assimilation to modernism) seem to have gone hand in hand. Their art modes (and mine) coincide historically with Diasporism in its most apparent modern posture and vulnerable time. Beckmann was not a Jew but he foretold, within free modernism, that a Diasporist art of painting would synthesize the perils, freedoms and all but unexplainable paradox of identity some of us would cleave to in art of our own. Diasporism may be more appropriate to paradox than even Surrealism was, because its life is lived while it is painted. The constraints and enigmas and brief freedoms of Diaspora are real as well as surreal.

Isaac Stern at Châtelet 1982

COMMONALITY

*What, then, of Kafka's cry that he could not feel any-
thing in common with himself, much less with Jews? The
question, of course, answers itself; the lowliest member
of Israel knows it for a 'Jewish' remark. Is it not, after
all, one of the things we may mean when we speak of
the Exile?*

found in an old journal of mine, unattributed

When I paint and draw, I often pretend to myself that I have
and want to have something in common with what I'm
picturing. We know now how much Kafka came to
share, 'in common', with Jews (he even tried Hebrew and
Zionism). He didn't get around to saying what he was
picturing – that would be left to thousands of others to
say when he was dead. But I don't mind saying a little
about what I paint, when I can . . . alive and fairly well.
I'm encourged in this, both by the Diasporist exegetical
tradition and the Diasporist tradition of rejection – in
this case rejection of the modern orthodox injunction
among painters, not to explain. And something (in common with myself?) compels me to *find*, as my (imagined)
Diasporist Picasso said we painters may do, what there
is, if anything, in Jewishness which I have in common

with other Jews and even whether Jewishness may be an attribute of art, as we hear, for instance, about the Englishness of English art. Kafka lived and died before the terrible Jewish Passion. Maybe he could smell it coming. Those painters who stood helpless in the Diaspora outside the stench of Europe have had, I believe, to mark well what transpired. For those whose ideas, painting ideas I mean, were clasped to the advent of a large, metaphysical art, abstraction for instance, the time may not have come ripe to announce the sombre turning in Jewishness clearly in painting. But they knew: Rothko knew, and that other cunning old Russian-American-Diasporist, Barnett Newman, he knew, when he said that the subject-matter of the artist is the most important thing to consider about his work. I knew them both in my youth. I think Newman meant the *Idea* was most important and the Idea has to mark the artist as he marks it. I, for one, can't believe that these men were not sensitized and conditioned *in their abstraction* by what was going on across the water and in their own milieux, during those very years when their art was emerging and Jewish history almost expired. My pictures are marked by Diasporist Ideas. Other artists have been maimed by them. It's all very well to say there's nothing in paintings except what you can see in them (like a pretty face?). I think the *Idea* is what counts. The Idea is the silver lining in art. Its character makes the art memorable. Trouble is, other people have got to *get* (receive) the Idea for a picture to stop them in their tracks and that doesn't have to happen at first glance, or ever. So we all *disagree* about pictures most of the time. A Diasporist picture is marked by Exile and its discontents as subtly

and unclearly as pictures painted by women or homosex-
uals are marked by their inner exilic discontents. If some
of us cover up (or raise up) our discontents in the name
of universalist art, I can see no reason why others
should not make memorable pictures in another name –
not 'art' but, say, (Diasporist) Commonality – as I choose
to believe Kafka did. And then it can be called art . . .
risen from universal connectedness. That is the meaning
of Schönberg's words: 'I have long since resolved to be a
Jew . . . I regard that as more important than my art.'

GOLDEN RULE

But they are a minority everywhere. They are constantly being made to look over their shoulders to see what other people think of them. Every Jew in every country experiences some degree of social uneasiness – I will not go further than that. No people can develop without distortion in an atmosphere of intermittent uneasiness. When people fidget, they are apt to irritate and be kicked, and because they are kicked, they fidget. It's a vicious circle.

Isaiah Berlin

I would reclaim the Jews and our little 'problem' for my corner of the painting art, when I can. A Diasporist painting is one in which a pariah people, an unpopular, stigmatized people, is taken up, pondered in their dilemmas, as unsurely as Impressionists ponder the dilemmas of light in nature or as Cubists take up perspectival and planar dilemmas. The Diasporist can paint a destiny in a face if he wills it so, if he can draw it, depict it, well enough so that it can be seen to be done, no easy thing to do. If I can't do it, some better painter will. Who is to say that a painted intimation of the (future) fate of someone depicted is less available to imaginative art than his (past) history is (in putative history-painting)? Van Gogh, who *may* not have been a Diasporist but was surely a related alien type, flitting here and there, sought to infuse his

Rock Garden (The Nation) 1981 (detail)

pictures with goodness (according to Meyer Shapiro). He wrote that Giotto faces were full of *kindness*. A Diasporist will find new ways to make pictures stand up for these old instincts in a world gone hateful again, that very world, shorn of Golden Rules, in which the Diasporist is never at home. Hillel (1st c. BCE) said: 'What is hateful to you, do not do to others.' This became the Diasporic Golden Rule, which is harder to achieve in life than, say, the expression (in art) of things like beauty, balance or anguish. The expression of kindness may be a very elusive and unusual painting factor, but I believe it belongs to art, and to Diasporist art. In my own time, which includes the Hitlerian and Stalinist genocides, and much else in that putrid lineage, I find myself in uneasy alliance with the natural pleasures of painting, which become conventional even as I do wish to pursue them, as one wishes to assimilate to agreeable milieux. This, then, is another Diasporist painting aspect (or mystery) – the marriage of conformity and the prospect of danger at the kindly altar of art, in a period like ours (unlike, say, 1912), when there is no revolutionary impulse, and good painters conform to the pleasures of paint. Diasporism is less mysterious in those various historical (and contested) Jewish proposals which offer both religious and secular dispositions, such as 'responsible alienation' (Pharisaism) and 'self-actualization', as concepts of purpose, defences through the ages, attempting to see some good in Exile. As a painter, I've come to detect something like moral power or destiny, living in more than one society, wrapped about in art, in its histories and antitheses. A recent critic of Diaspora values called this 'psycho-aesthetic indulgence' and 'solipsistic self-satisfaction

Rock Garden (The Nation) 1981 (detail)

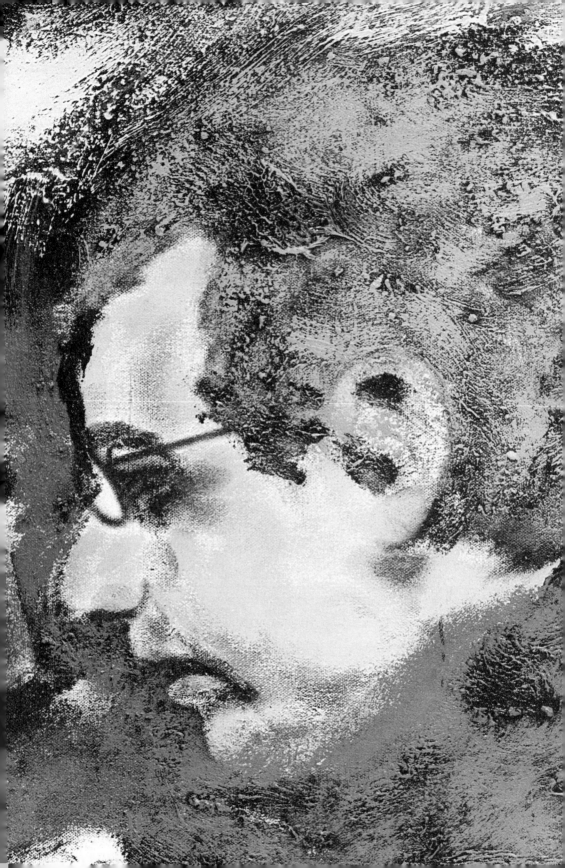

through an act of existential defiance' – wow! There's more to this than meets the eye, and it circles back to the *mitzvah* (commandment) of kindness in a schizophrenic way, which I will try to take up in my Second Diasporist Manifesto, if there is to be one; the hubristic Diasporist rides again?

Rock Garden (The Nation) 1981 (detail)

AFTER 1945

Why the children in the gas chambers?

Primo Levi

After 1945, the world changed for the Jews. If your world
changes, your paintings change. Your hand, changed by
heart and mind, goes at its tasks in new ways. Of
course, I only mean those painters who have been affected, those who don't refuse my idea that their world
changed after 1945. In that version of Diasporist painting
within which I pretend to speak, each of us reflects only
upon our own singular reactions to what we learn about
the events of 1940–45, from one vantage place or another. The great tried and true aspects of our painting
art we attempt to preserve – those eternal, hard-fought
sanities like formal and thematic daring and invention,
probing drawing skills, touch and gesture, experiment,
delight in paint and color, reverence for pictures by other
artists, and so on. We (I) try and fail at these things as

The Jewish School (Drawing a Golem) 1980 (detail)

we try and fail at versions of morality in our lives, but may I suggest that some Diasporist art addresses, as well as these other things, a stunned amazement upon learning the events preceding 1945? *Diasporist art finds itself transplanted by these events and their elusive meaning*; here I paraphrase Primo Levi who was describing Auschwitz to Philip Roth, two great Diasporists. Levi says: 'I had an intense wish to understand, I was constantly pervaded by a curiosity that somebody afterwards did, in fact, deem nothing less than cynical: the curiosity of the naturalist who finds himself transplanted into an environment that is monstrous, but new, monstrously new.' After 1945 (Jewish) Diasporist painting makes it new because it has new things to face, events never faced before, a profoundly different world-view, an art to remodel. According to Martin Buber (1878–1965), the innermost meaning of that event was a message from God for a turning and a renewal. I thought the message from God had not reached me yet but since my art has turned and renewed itself, maybe I got the message after all.

Yiddish Hamlet 1985

THE ROMANTIC JEW
(ANCESTRAL HOUSES)

Kafka wins through to an intuition of the Jewish condi-
tion in the Diaspora so vivid as to convert the expression
of itself into an integral part of itself; so complete, that
is, that the intuition becomes Jewish in style as well as
in sense . . . the only example I know of an integrally
Jewish literary art that is fully at home in a modern Gen-
tile language.

Clement Greenberg

Much of my life I've been a good bad boy. I've pursued the
Spirit of Romance as good bad boys do in Art and Life. I
chased it all over Europe, across America, into and out
of trouble and assimilations of many kinds. I've become
an Honorary Englishman, a Suspicious Reader, A Dissident from homogenizing mainstreams, with a craving for
what Flaubert called the 'bitter undertaste' of city
streets. Sometimes I think I caught the Spirit of Romance
in my little net for a moment or two. Mostly I failed at it.
My Absurdist painting, upon which I lavish the meager
Romance fluttering in my net, has suffered complainingly
at the aging cosmopolite I've become, blotting my copybook, roundly cursed. But wait! These pursuits, this dubious Romance may prove more fateful than forlorn as
the suspicion arises I've been making my way through

The Jew, Etc. (First State) 1976

ancestral houses all the while – Diaspora Jewry haunts those places and moments where I sought out the art of Romance and I only began to know that and myself in recent years. Diasporism is a Romance as cunning as one's Homeland is. Diasporism in the oddly persistent easel-painting we fashion for ourselves *will* convert the expression of itself, as Greenberg suggests (if one wins through!). Being what one is translates into doing what one does on canvas anyway. And it seems to me appropriate to the way romantic easel-painting persists, that it should be Diasporist in style and in sense, that the weird persistence of a Jewish nation (against all odds) can suggest a refulgence, unexpected and even resisted in art, among dispersed, very conflicting, menaced Jewry. I say, against friendly and not so friendly advice, that a universal cart can be driven by a new, untried, particular, idiosyncratic horse. It's been done before.

Bather (Frankfurt) 1985

DIASPORIST TRADITION

Being elsewhere, the great vice of this race, the great secret virtue, the great vocation of this people.

Charles Peguy (on the Jews)

For some years now, I've been trying to make out the traditions to which I belong. I've watched other painters doing the same thing. Most of them seem to me to have resolved mainly to belong to art itself – not a bad thing at all, to belong to the history and traditions of abstraction or to the even more generic tradition of avant-gardeism, the tradition of the new, 'advancing' painting in one way or another. Others seem to wish to belong to a profound European painting tradition which runs from late Titian, through Rembrandt and beyond Cézanne to one's own special anxieties (as I often wish to do myself). Some American artists, some very hard ones, have spoken openly of belonging to an American tradition which, in its advanced posture, jettisons Europe. As in poetry (Yeats: 'We Irish, born into that ancient sect'), music and

other practices, there are painters who find themselves happily in national traditions. Picasso made himself at home in and belonged to many of these things and devoured them for breakfast (even Diasporism). Negation of the pre-Hitler Diaspora of uprooting expulsion and catastrophe trailing back to the Book of Lamentations, advocated by the very attractive agnostic Ahad Ha'am, in a version of cultural nationalism, proved to be a precious escape from the Dark Age in which many Jews were still buried then (in his time). Ahad Ha'am may be to the Diasporist of 1912 what Cézanne was to the Cubist of 1912. I wonder if he ever heard of Cézanne. They are both lighthouses, even bridges for me in 1987. I'm still trying to learn an affirmative painting art. In fact I like to think of composing or structuring pictures in defiance of that contraction of the (Jewish) national 'ego' Ahad Ha'am saw as the major negative aspect of Diaspora. And so I've come to make myself a tradition in that Diaspora, until I can think of a better place, where the terms of my own life have been staged. It is as a real American rootless Jew, riddled with assimilationist secularism and Anglophiliac-Europist art mania, besieged by modernisms and their skeptical overflow, fearful at the prospect and state of Wandering, un-at-homeness, yet unable to give myself to Ohio or God or Israel or London or California. Like Kafka, I've never made a frank deposit into the Bank of Belief; not yet, but I've come in recent years to study myself into my oversized Diasporist shoes, to discover and invent Diasporism as a painting art mode, to realize where and how I belong to this instant age-old tradition, and feel sometimes, on a good day, it knocks my socks off, as Cubism must have done to the Cubists.

Bather (Psychotic Boy) 1980 (detail)

THE ALMOND TREE

This 'being elsewhere' combined with the desperate wish to 'be at home' in a manner at once intense, fruitful and destructive.

Gershom Scholem (on Jews and Germans)

Within my Diasporist painting mode there appeared a Morbid Period, during which days on end were depressed in a lachrymose, self-inflicted momentum of reading and brooding over the events of the National Socialist hell (my zero-point of history). Painters have pondered hell (based on reading) in their pictures before, but the life-spark of art is frail enough in most of us and I remain fearful for the life of paintings made upon the shadows of such spectres as the burning alive of children in front of their parents' eyes, which will curdle my last painting day on earth. This Morbid Period grew to seem to fit the span of my own life, from the year of my birth in Ohio (and Hitler's rise), to the present daily refulgence of Jew-Hatred with its focus on Israel and its promise of yet another bloody Jewish Dispersion. Strong as she seems (?),

Passion (1940–45) Reading 1985

ADEN-ARABIE

Israel (which someone called a state born from a historical encounter with doomsday) has been too small, imperilled, unlucky and often poorly run to avoid the kind of awful suppression of Arab people which has led to a hated Diaspora for the Palestinian and God knows what in store for Israel. They both need separate homes. The idea of a bi-national secular state in Palestine can only happen in a month of Sundays, draped in blood. As humans go, it's hopeless.

I always keep a picture, tacked to my wall, of the gorgeous little painting of the Almond Tree which Bonnard was working at on his last day, to remind me of another fate, a more sublime and fixed one than that of Jews or my own peculiar Diasporism, where painting marks on canvas may spell peripatetic danger instead of peace in the sun. In fact, I return this day to a tiny picture of a False Messiah I thought I'd finished, taking up Bonnard's little tree, to infuse my Messiah with hopeful white paint, befitting the End of Days, prolonging its poor prospects and smothering the negative constraints of Diaspora for a moment; those negative aspects by the way, which in traditional interpretations are due to be resolved in the messianic end of time. I just came across a Biblical allusion to the flowering almond interpreted as the white head of an old man . . . so my poor Messiah can be aged and maybe even something more than false.

Aden-Arabie 1969

ERROR

I am a stranger and a sojourner.

Abraham

Having thought up the term Diasporism for painting, I now
think it may be a name for the unnamable. It concerns
me that my own painting modes, once I 'identify' with
the worldly mode of dispersion, and in half-flight from
the habits of my aesthetic hosts, shall lead to a place of
no rest. Matisse wanted to achieve a place of rest (of
composure?). But Cézanne? I hope not . . . there is evidence enough he did not wish to conclude pictures with
impunity, evidence pointing to what Maurice Blanchot
(b. 1907) called 'the infinite migration of error'. Then
Blanchot explains me and my painting to myself: 'Error
means wandering, the inability to abide and stay. . . .
The wanderer's country is not truth, but exile; he lives
outside.'

Hamlet's Ghost (The King of Denmark) 1985 (detail)

It is this unsettled and unsettling state of art which Diasporism, if it exists, fails to resolve – and even that, fitfully. But I want to believe in its future tense.

Kitaj and Sandra Fisher, Marriage (Synagogue of the Spanish Jews, London, 15 December 1983; photo by David Hockney)

GLOSSARY OF NAMES AND TERMS

AHAD HA'AM (1856–1927): pseudonym of Asher Ginzberg. For him the sovereignty of the Jewish people under international law was less important than having a cultural centre of Judaism in Palestine – cultural Zionism.

ADORNO, THEODOR W. (1903–69): philosopher and sociologist. The main representative of the Frankfurt school together with Horkheimer.

AKIBA (AD 50–c. 136): rabbi. Studied for 24 years before feeling called to be a teacher. He died a martyr's death during the persecution of the Jews by Hadrian.

Aliyah: Hebrew for pulling up. Since 1882 an expression for the immigration to Palestine, or rather Israel. Here: ascent.

BAECK, LEO (1873–1956): religious philosopher and rabbi. He followed his congregation into the Theresienstadt concentration camp of his own free will and survived. As a follower of Kant he refused Hasidism and supported a progressive Judaism.

BENJAMIN, WALTER (1892–1940): German writer, literary critic, and social philosopher. He committed suicide at the Spanish border while on the run from the Gestapo.

BERLIN, ISAIAH (b. 1909): political scientist and philosopher at Oxford University. Works include: *Karl Marx* (1939), *The Age of Enlightenment* (1956), *History and Theory* (1960).

BLACKMUR, R. P. (1904–65): American poet and critic.

BLANCHOT, MAURICE (b. 1907): French writer of novels and short stories as well as of literary criticism and essays.

BOMBERG, DAVID (1890–1957): English painter who, as a contemporary of the Vorticists (*c.* 1915), started off painting strongly geometrical compositions of figures; later works were expressive and many-layered. Taught Frank Auerbach and Leon Kossoff.

BUBER, MARTIN (1878–1965): religious philosopher. From 1923 to 1933 professor at the university of Frankfurt. One of the leading Zionists who tried to revive Jewish mysticism, principally through translation and interpretation of the Hasidic books. Worked for peace with Arabs.

Cheder: Hebrew for a study or room. Classroom of the Jewish primary school for children (from the ages of 4 to 13).

DUBNOW, SIMON (1860–1941, murdered by the Nazis): historian. He saw in autonomy the driving force behind Jewish history. Leading Diasporist.

FACKENHEIM, EMIL (b. 1916): rabbi and professor of philosophy in Toronto. He argued that after the Holocaust the law of survival was added as number 614 to the known 613 commandments.

Galut: Hebrew for banishment or deportation. An expression for the exile and the diaspora. Its history begins with the destruction of the Second Temple (AD 70).

HEINE, HEINRICH (1797–1856): German poet and critic who converted to Christianity (1825). Works include: *Gedichte* (1822), *Buch der Lieder* (1827), *Reisebilder* (1826–31), *Romantische Schule* (1836), *Neue Gedichte* (1844) and *Romanzero* (1951).

HILLEL: rabbi and teacher in Jerusalem *c.* 30 BC. Supporter of a more lenient, practical interpretation of the law.

MASADA: Herod's palace-fortress to the west of the Dead Sea; after the fall of Jerusalem in AD 70 it was defended against the Roman besiegers for three years by Jewish patriots who eventually committed mass suicide. A symbol of danger but also of the Jewish desire for freedom.

Midrash: Hebrew for, literally, interpretation of the Bible. A talk concerning the readings from the Torah and the literature that has arisen from it. Here: explanation, interpretation of the meaning passed on.

Mitzvah: Hebrew for God's commandment, religious duty, good deed, law.

PINSKER, LEO (1821–91): doctor and propagandist. He considered anti-semitism an insufferable condition that could only be cured by national independence. He wrote *Auto-Emancipation: an exhortation by a Russian Jew to his Jewish comrades* (1882).

Responsa: in Hebrew *teshuvot*. Legal questions put to rabbis and their considered responses; the equivalent of case law.

SAXL, FRITZ (1890–1948): Viennese art historian, director of the Warburg Institute in 1929. Works include: *Antiker Götter in der Spätrenaissance, Pagan Sacrifice in the Italian Renaissance* and *A Spiritual Encyclopaedia of the Later Middle Ages*.

SCHOOL OF LONDON: Kitaj used this term for the first time in 1976 when he organized the exhibition 'The Human Clay'. It is a loose designation to describe various painters then working in London, including Bacon, Freud, Hockney, Blake, Auerbach, Hodgkin, Kossoff, Andrews, Kitaj and quite a few others.

Sefirot: kabbalistic presentation of ten creative powers of the divine (crown, wisdom, reason, greatness, strength, beauty, continuity, majesty, foundations, kingdom). Here: according to the teaching of the kabbalah, emanations and the essence of the spirit which embody the divine.

Shoah: destruction. New Hebrew term for the Holocaust.

SINGER, JOE: a friend of Kitaj's family, and a figure in his paintings and drawings.

Talmud: study, explanation. According to the Bible, the main work of Judaism which was completed around AD 500.

WARBURG, ABY (1866–1929): German art historian, whose art library was moved from Hamburg to London in 1933 and later became the Warburg Institute, University of London. He was interested in the religious, astrological, psychological and superstitious contexts of works of art.

WIND, EDGAR (1900–71): German-born British art historian, deputy director of the Warburg Institute and honorary lecturer in philosophy at University College, London, 1934–42. He taught in America and in 1955 became professor of history of art at Oxford University, until 1967. Works include: *Pagan Mysteries in the Renaissance* (1958) and *Art and Anarchy* (1963). Wind and Kitaj were friendly in Oxford.

Zaddik: the righteous, the miracle worker. *Zaddikim* were leaders of Hasidism to whom the believers turned in order to achieve a state of rapture while praying.

ZANGWILL, ISRAEL (1864–1926): writer. At first a Zionist, later founder of the International Jewish Territorial Organization. Author of *Children of the Ghetto* (1892).

Zohar: Hebrew for (book of) splendor, one of the principle works of Jewish mysticism.